HAL•LEONARD®

DRUM
PLAY-ALONG

AUDIO
ACCESS
INCLUDED

PLAYBACK+
Speed • Pitch • Balance • Loop

VOL. 3

HARD ROCK

To access audio visit:
www.halleonard.com/mylibrary

Enter Code
6305-7073-3714-9985

Tracking, mixing, and mastering by Jake Johnson
Drums by Scott Schroedl
Guitars by Doug Boduch
Bass by Tom McGirr
Keyboards by Warren Wiegratz

ISBN 978-1-4234-0428-6

HAL•LEONARD®

7777 W. BLUEMOUND RD. P.O. BOX 13819 MILWAUKEE, WI 53213

Visit Hal Leonard Online at
www.halleonard.com

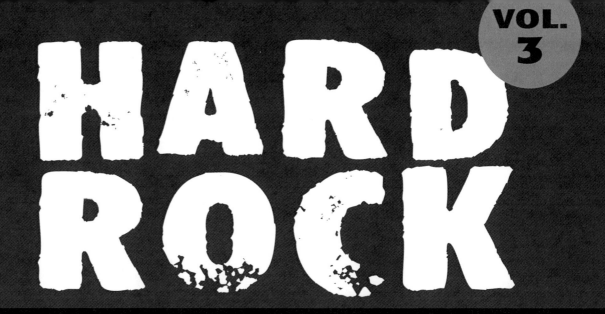

HAL•LEONARD®
DRUM
PLAY-ALONG

AUDIO
ACCESS
INCLUDED

VOL.
3

HARD
ROCK

CONTENTS

Bark at the Moon

Words and Music by Ozzy Osbourne

Intro
Moderate Rock ♩ = 148

Verse

1. Screams   break   the si - lence.   Wak - ing   from   the   dead   of   night.

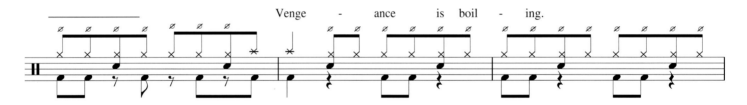

Venge - ance   is   boil - ing.

He's re - turned to kill   the   light. _____   Then   when he's _____

Pre-Chorus

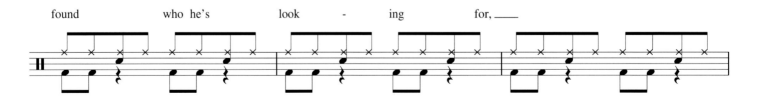

found   who he's   look - ing   for, ____

lis - ten in_____ awe and you'll hear_____ him

Interlude

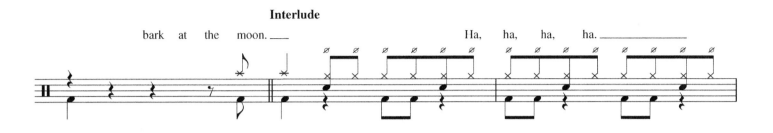

bark at the moon. ___ Ha, ha, ha, ha. _____

_____ Now he has ris - en.

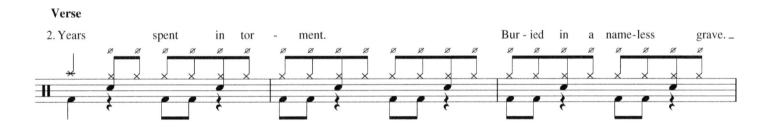

Verse

2. Years spent in tor - ment. Bur - ied in a name-less grave. _

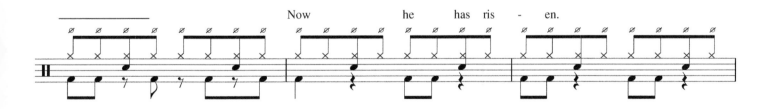

Pre-Chorus

Mir - a - cles would have to save. _____ Those that the

beast   is   look   -   ing   for, ___

lis   -   ten   in ___ awe   and   you'll   hear _____ him

Chorus

bark   at   the   moon. ___

Hey, _____   yeah,   bark   at   the   moon. _

Bridge
Half-time feel

They   cursed   and   bur   -   ied   him,   a   -   long   with ___ shame. _

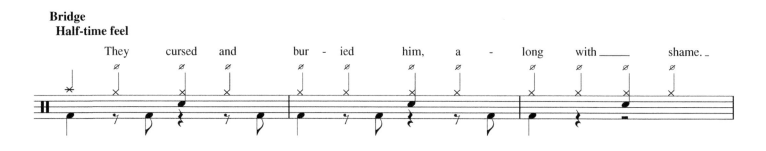

And   thought   his   time - less   soul   had

Interlude

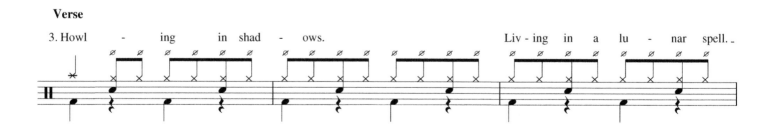

Verse

3. Howl - ing   in shad - ows.   Liv - ing   in   a   lu - nar spell.

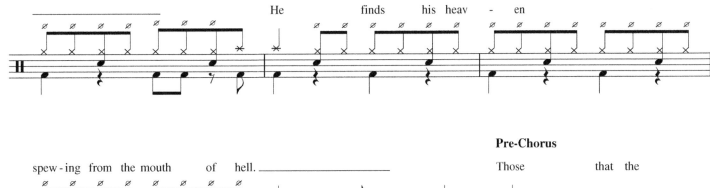

He finds his heav - en

spew-ing from the mouth of hell.

Pre-Chorus

Those that the

beast is look - ing for, ____

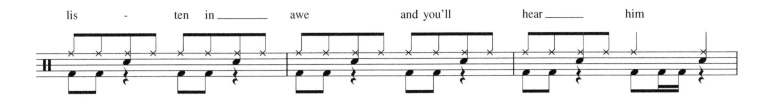

lis - ten in ____ awe and you'll hear ____ him

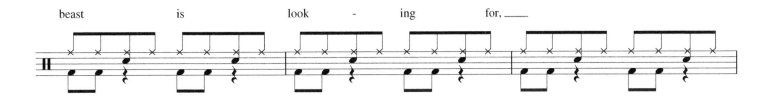

Chorus

bark at the moon. ____

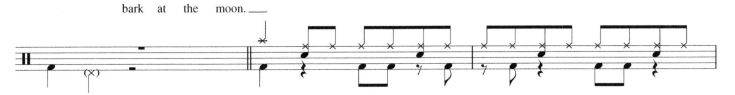

Hey, ____ yeah, bark at the moon. ____

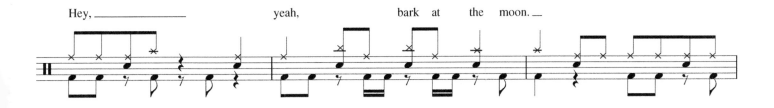

Hey, ____ yeah, bark at the moon. ____

Oh, _____

yeah, __   bark   at   the   moon.

Outro

Ow! _____

Detroit Rock City

Words and Music by Paul Stanley and Bob Ezrin

I hear my song, __ and it

pulls me through. __

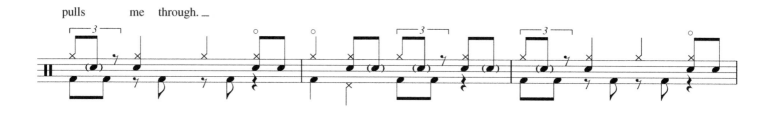

Comes on strong; tells me what I got to do. _____ I got _

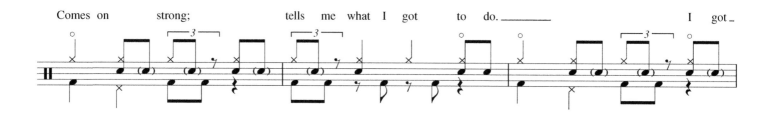

Chorus

__ to get up! Ev -'ry - bod - y's gon - na move their feet. Get down! _

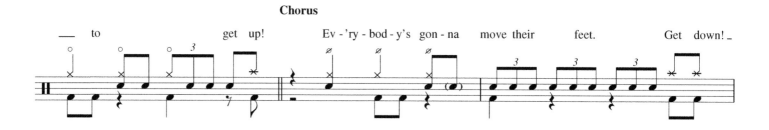

__ Ev -'ry - bod - y's gon - na leave their seat. _____ You

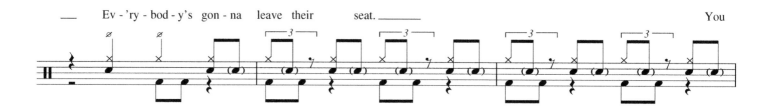

got - ta lose your mind in De - troit Rock Cit - y. Get up! _

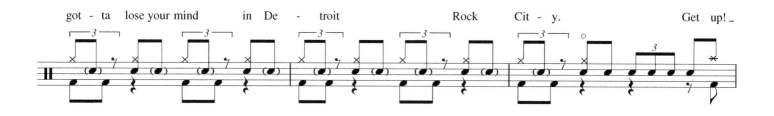

__ Ev -'ry - bod - y's gon - na move their feet. Get down! _ Ev -'ry - bod - y's gon - na

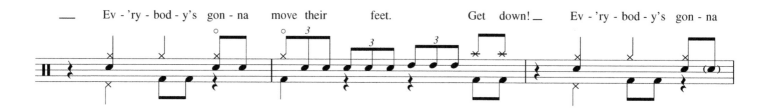

Verse

leave their   seat._____   2. Get - tin'   late, _   I   just can't   wait.

Ten o' - clock, _   and I

know   I   got - ta hit   the   road. _____

First I   drink,   then   I   smoke.

Start up the car, _   and I   try to make the mid - night   show. _

Chorus

_____   Get up! ___   Ev - 'ry - bod - y's gon - na

move their   feet.   Get down! _ Ev - 'ry - bod - y's gon - na leave their   seat. _____

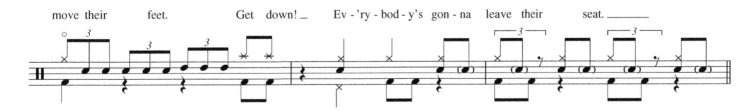

Interlude

Verse

3. Mov - in'   fast __   down

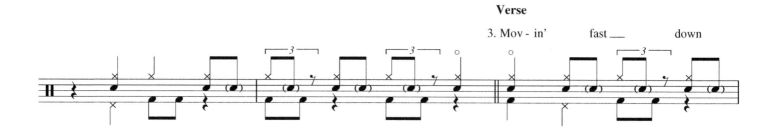

Nine - ty - Five. __

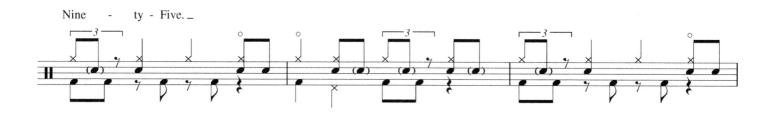

Hit top speed, ___ but I'm still mov - in' much too slow. _____

I feel so good; I'm so a - live. ___

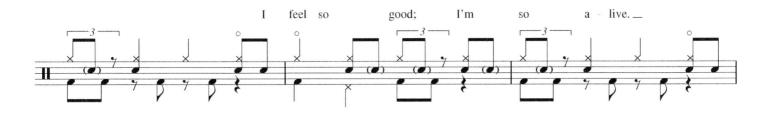

Hear my song ___

play - in' on the ra - di - o. _____ It goes: ___ Get up! ___

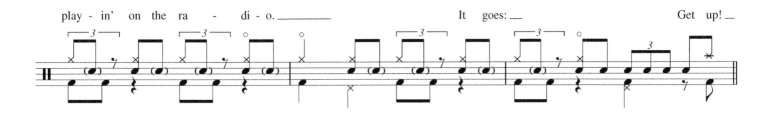

Chorus

___ Ev - 'ry - bod - y's gon - na move their feet. Get down! ___ Ev - 'ry - bod - y's gon - na

leave their seat. _____

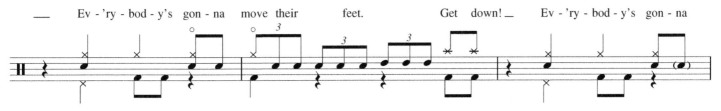

Interlude

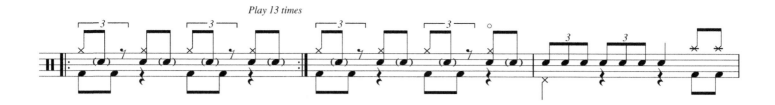

You got - ta lose your life in De -

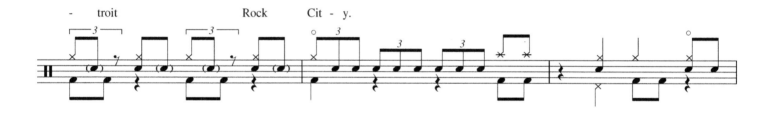

- troit Rock Cit - y.

Verse

4. Twelve o' - clock, ___ I got - ta rock. ___

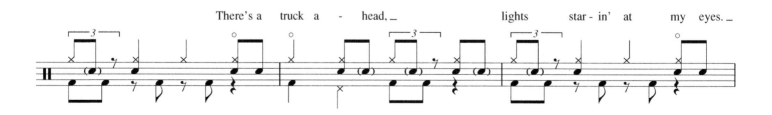

There's a truck a - head, ___ lights star - in' at my eyes. ___

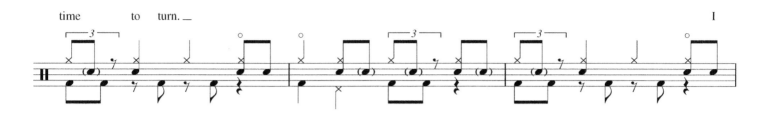

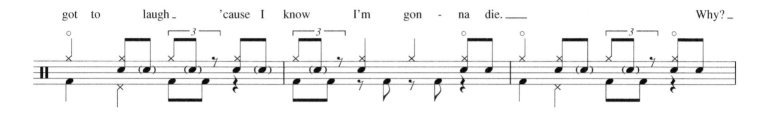

Chorus

Living After Midnight

Words and Music by Glenn Tipton, Rob Halford and K.K. Downing

1. I took the cit - y 'bout a   one A.   M. ___   Load - ed,   load -
2. Got gleam - in' chrome   re - flect - ing   feel. ___   Load - ed,   load -
3. The air's e - lec - tric,   spark - in'   pow - er.   Load - ed,   load -

- ed.   I'm all geared up   to   score   a - gain. ___   Load -
- ed.   Read - y to take on   ev - 'ry   deal. ___   Load -
- ed.   I'm get - tin' hard - er   by ___ the   hour. ___   Load -

- ed,   load - ed.
- ed,   load - ed.
- ed,   load - ed.

Pre-Chorus

I come a - live   in the
My pulse is rac - in',
I   set   my   sights   and then _

To Coda ⊕

2nd time, substitute Fill 1
3rd time, substitute Fill 2

ne - on   lights. _   That's   when   I   make   my   moves ___   right. _ ⎱
hot to   take. _   But this   mo - tor's   revved _   up,   fit ___   to   break. _ ⎰
___ home   in. ___   The   joint _   starts   fly'n' ___   when   I ___   be - gin. ___

Chorus

Liv - in'   af - ter   mid - night,   rock - in'   to   the
___

Fill 1

Fill 2

dawn.   Lov - in'   till   the   morn - in',   then I'm   gone, _

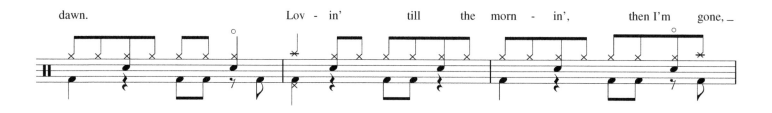

‾‾   I'm   gone. _

    ⌐1.   ⌐2.

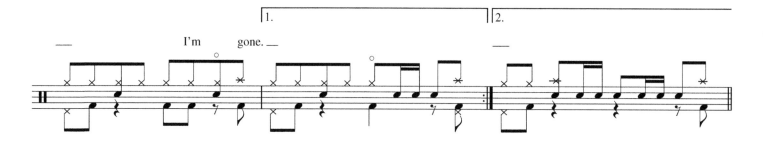

Bridge

I'm _____ aim -

- in'   for ___ ya.   I'm _

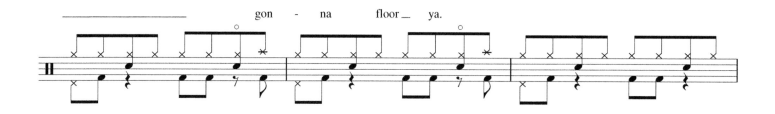

_____   gon - na   floor _ ya.

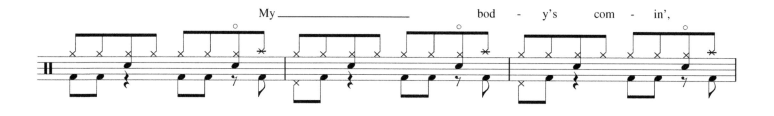

My _____   bod - y's   com - in',

all _____   night _

Guitar Solo

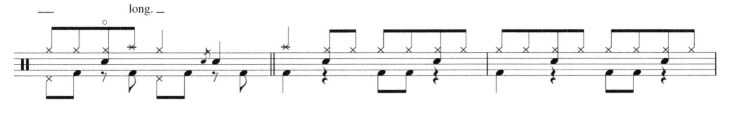

D.S. al Coda

$\oplus$ **Coda**

$\%\ \%$ **Outro-Chorus**

Liv - in'   af - ter   mid - night,   rock - in'   to   the

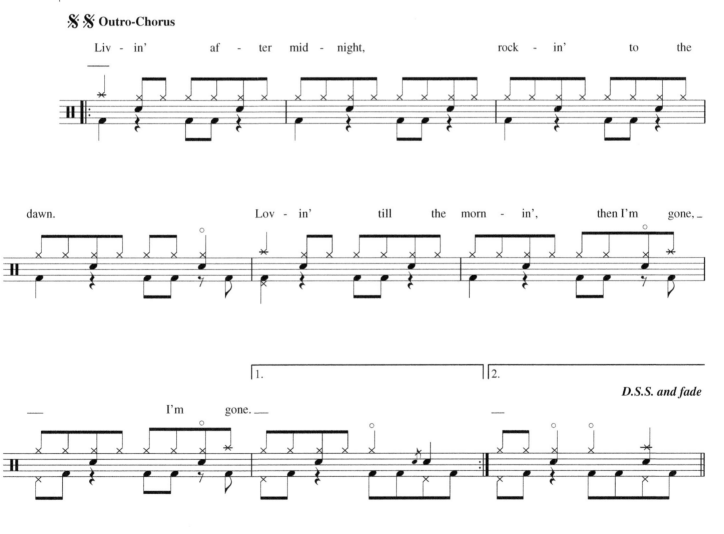

dawn.   Lov - in'   till   the   morn - in',   then I'm   gone, __

|1. |2.

D.S.S. and fade

__   I'm   gone. __

Panama

Words and Music by David Lee Roth, Edward Van Halen and Alex Van Halen

Intro
Moderate Rock ♩ = 144

Oo!   Oh, ___

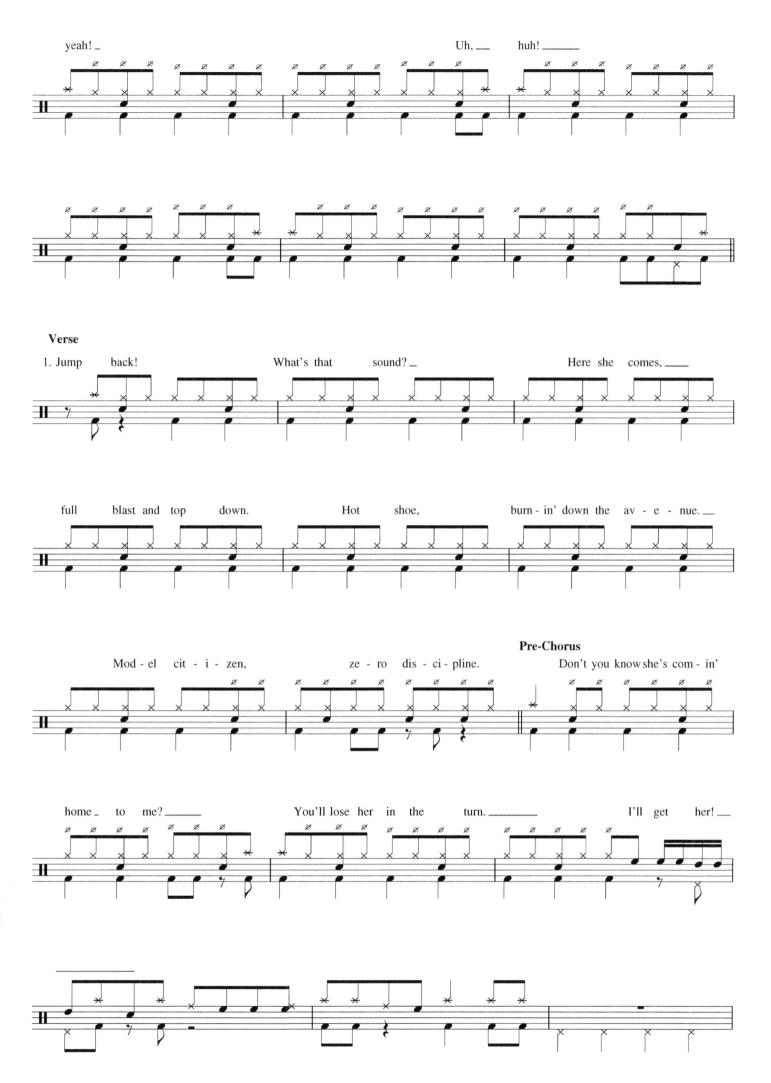

Chorus

Verse

Pre-Chorus

Outro-Chorus

Rock You Like a Hurricane

Words and Music by Herman Rarebell, Klaus Meine and Rudolf Schenker

Intro
Moderate Rock ♩ = 124

(Guitar)

1. It's

Verse

ear - ly   morn - ing,   the   sun comes   out. ___   Last   night was   shak - ing   and

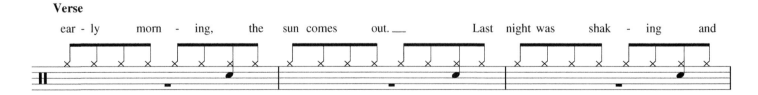

hur - ri - cane. _____ 2. My

𝄋 Verse

bod - y is burn - ing, it starts to shout. _ De - sire's ___ com - ing, it
ear - ly morn - ing, the sun comes out. ___ Last night was shak - ing and

breaks out loud. __ Lust is in cag - es, 'til storm breaks loose. _____ Just
real - ly loud. __ My cat is pur - ring; it scratched my skin. _ So,

2nd time, substitute Fill 1

have to make __ it with some - one I choose. _
what is wrong _ with an - oth - er sin? ____

The night is call - ing, I

have to go. _____ The wolf is hun - gry, he runs the show. _ He's

Fill 1

Chorus

hur - ri - cane. _____ Rock _ you like a

Guitar Solo

hur - ri - cane.

D.S. al Coda

3. It's

⊕ Coda

Outro-Chorus

love at first sting. ____

Here I am, rock ____ you like a

hur - ri - cane. Are you read - y, ba - by? ____ Here I am,

rock ____ you like a hur - ri - cane. ____

Here I am, rock ____ you like a hur - ri - cane. Well,

come on, come on, come on, ___ come on, come on. Here I am, rock ____ you like a

hur - ri - cane. ____ Here I am.

Run to the Hills

Words and Music by Steven Harris

LEGEND

Drummer: Clive Burr

Intro
Moderate Rock ♩ = 120

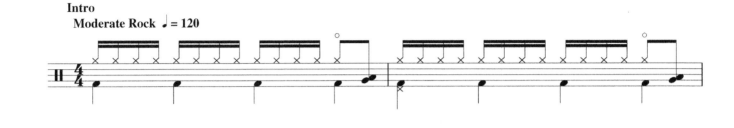

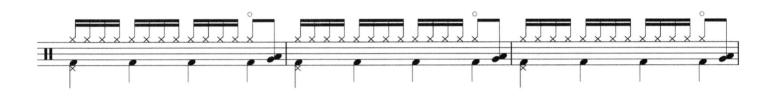

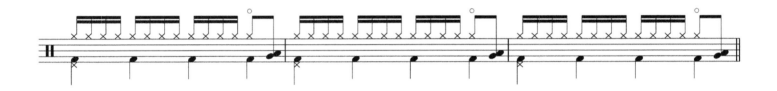

Verse

1. White man ___ came ___ a - cross the ___ sea, ___ he
   fought him ___ hard, ___ we fought him _ well, ___ out

brought us ___ pain ___ and mis - er - y. ___ He
on the ___ plains ___ we gave him hell. ___ But

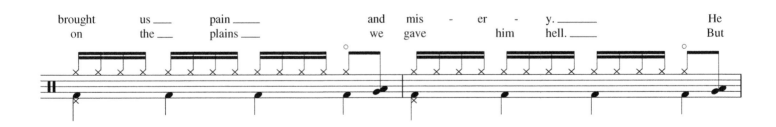

killed   our __   tribes, ___   he   killed   our __   creed, ___   he
man - y _____   came, ___   too   much   for the __   Cree, ___   oh,

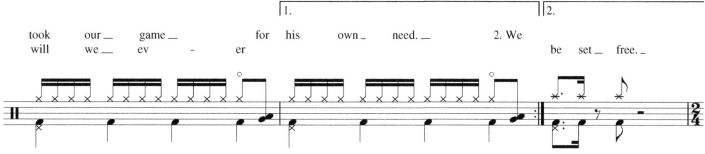

|1.

|2.

took   our __   game __   for   his   own _   need. __   2. We
will   we __   ev -   er   be   set _   free. _

Faster ♩ = 172

Verse

3. Rid -   ing   through   dust   clouds   and   bar - ren   wastes, __
4. Sol -   dier   blue   in   the   bar - ren   wastes, __

gal - lop -   ing   hard   on   the   plains. __
hunt - ing   and   kill - ing's   a   game.

Chas - ing   the   red - skins   back   to   their   holes,
Rap - ing   the   wom - en   and   wast - ing   the   men,   the

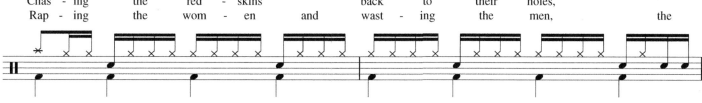

fight - ing them at their own game. _____
on - ly good in - juns are tame.

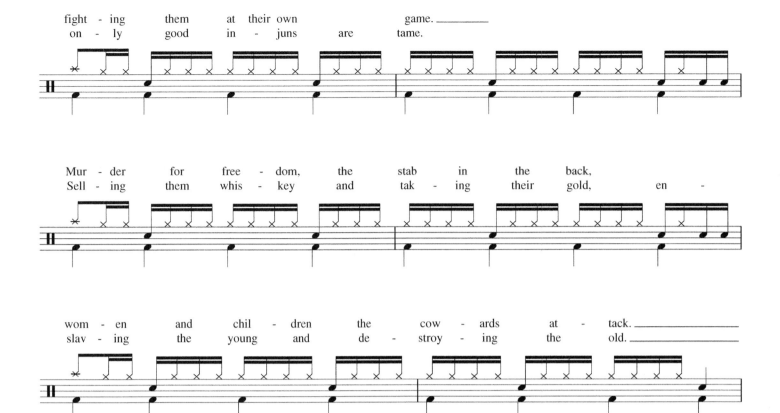

Mur - der for free - dom, the stab in the back,
Sell - ing them whis - key and tak - ing their gold, en -

wom - en and chil - dren the cow - ards at - tack. _____
slav - ing the young and de - stroy - ing the old. _____

Chorus

Run to the

hills, run

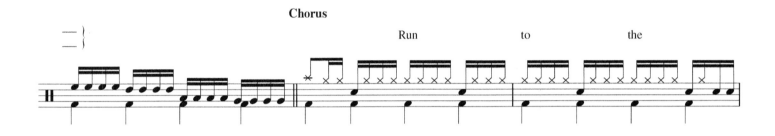

for _____ your lives. _____

Run to the hills,

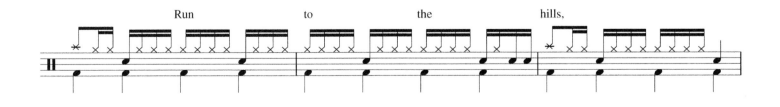

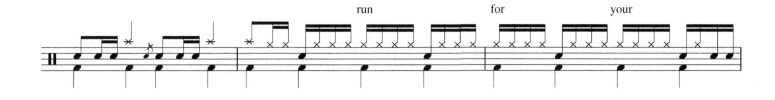

run   for   your

1.   2.

lives.   lives.

Guitar Solo

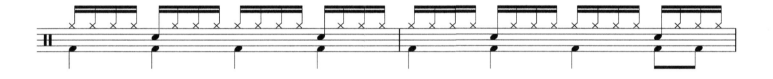

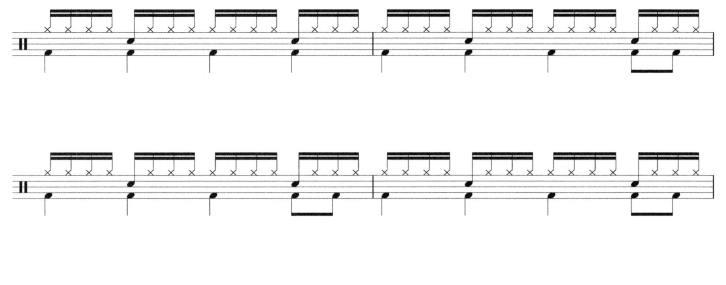

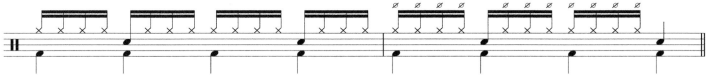

Interlude

Yeah, _____

Play 8 times

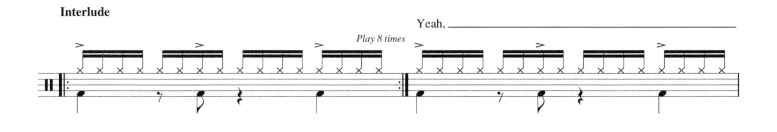

ah. _____

gradually open

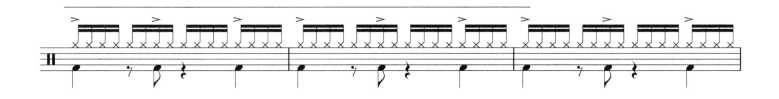

Chorus

Ah! _____   Run   to   the

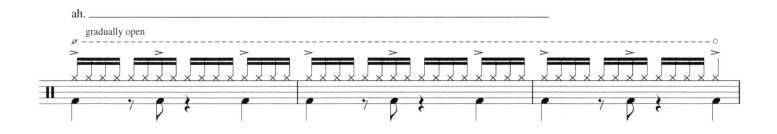

hills,   run

for _____ your   lives. _____

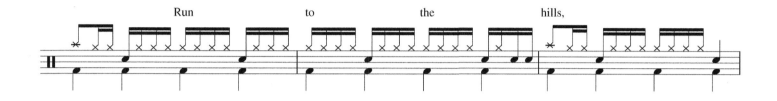

Run   to   the   hills,

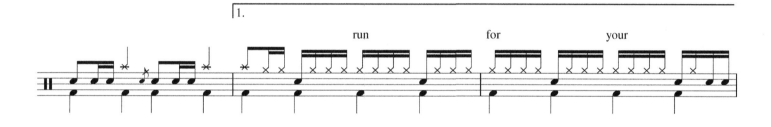

1.
                                   run   for   your

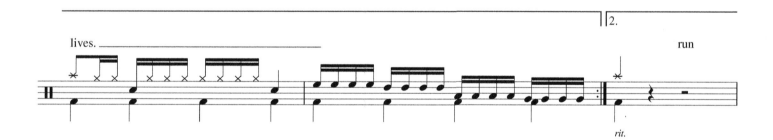

2.
lives. _____   run

rit.

Free time

for   your   life. _____   Ah!

rit.

Smoke on the Water

Words and Music by Ritchie Blackmore, Ian Gillan,
Roger Glover, Jon Lord and Ian Paice

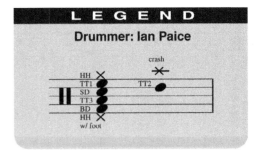

Intro
Moderate Rock ♩ = 112

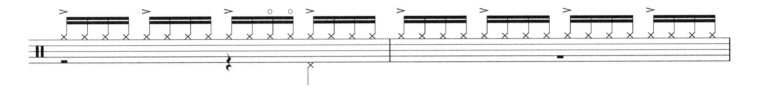

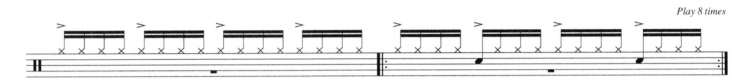

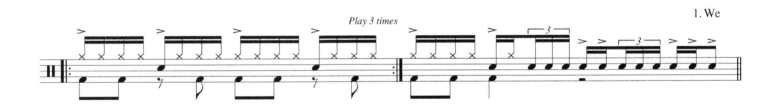

Verse

all came out to Mon - treaux   on the Lake __ Ge - ne - va shore -

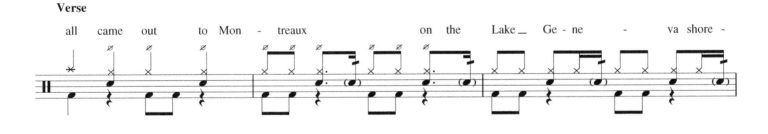

- line   to make   re - cords with the   mo - bile, _____

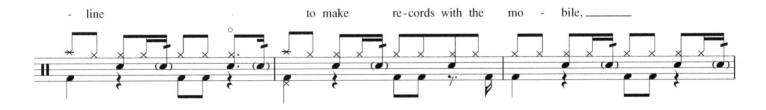

we did-n't have much time.___ But Frank Zap-pa and the

Moth - ers _____ were at the best place a - round. ___

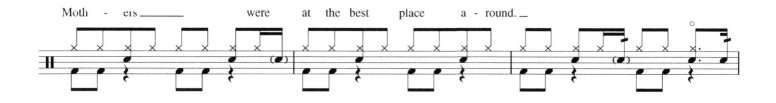

But some stu-pid with a flare gun burned the place to the ___ ground. _

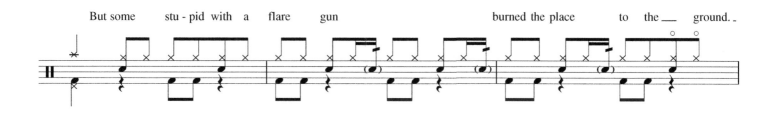

Chorus

Smoke on the wa - ter,

a fire ___ in the sky. ___ Smoke on the

wa - ter.

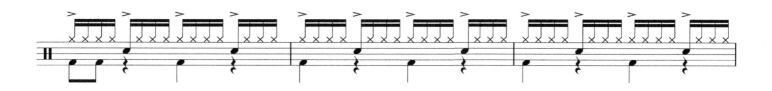

Verse

2. They burned down the gam - bling house, __ it died with an aw - ful sound. __

__ A Funk - y Claude was run - ning in and out, __

pull - ing kids out the ground. __ When it all was o -

- ver, __ we had to find an - oth - er place. __

But Swiss time was run - ning out; it seemed that we would lose the race. __

Chorus

__ Smoke on the wa - ter,

a fire___ in the sky.___ Smoke on the

wa - ter.

Play 6 times

Guitar Solo

Play 6 times

Play 6 times

Verse

3. We end-ed up at the Grand Ho-tel, _____ it was emp - ty,

cold   and bare.   But with   the   Roll-ing truck   Stones   thing   just   out - side,

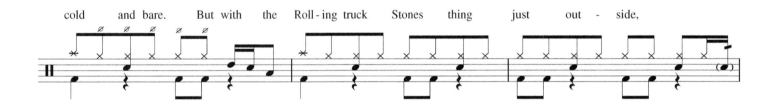

mak-ing our   mu - sic   there. _   With   a   few red   lights,   a

few old   beds _   we made a   place   to   sweat. _

No mat - ter   what   we   get out of this,   I know,   I know we'll

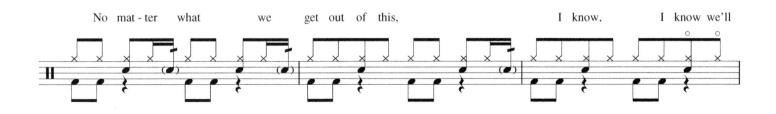

Chorus

nev - er for - get.   Smoke   on the   wa -   ter,

a fire ___ in the sky. ___   Smoke   on the

Outro

wa -   ter.   *Play 7 times*

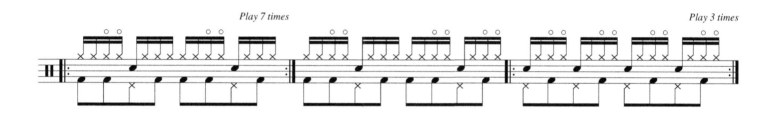

Play 7 times   *Play 3 times*

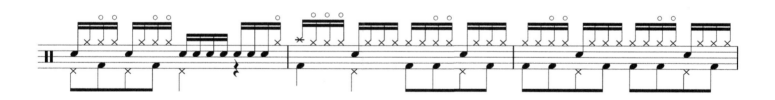

Begin fade

Fade out

War Pigs
(Interpolating Luke's Wall)

Words and Music by Frank Iommi, John Osbourne,
William Ward and Terence Butler

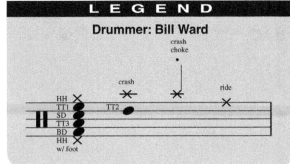

Interlude

Interlude

Bridge

Pol - i - ti - cian's hide them - selves a - way, they on - ly start - ed the war.

Why should they go out

to fight? They leave that all to the poor. Yeah.

Interlude

Bridge

Time will tell _ on their _ pow - er _ minds, _

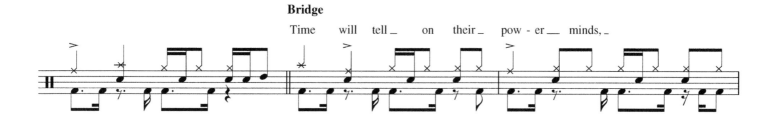

mak - ing war _ just for fun. _

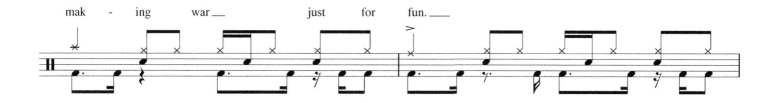

Treat - ing peo - ple just like pawns in _ chess, _

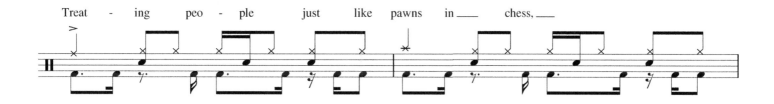

wait till their judge - ment day _ comes. _ Yeah. _

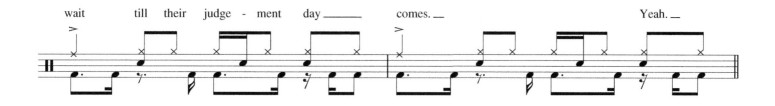

Interlude

Guitar Solo

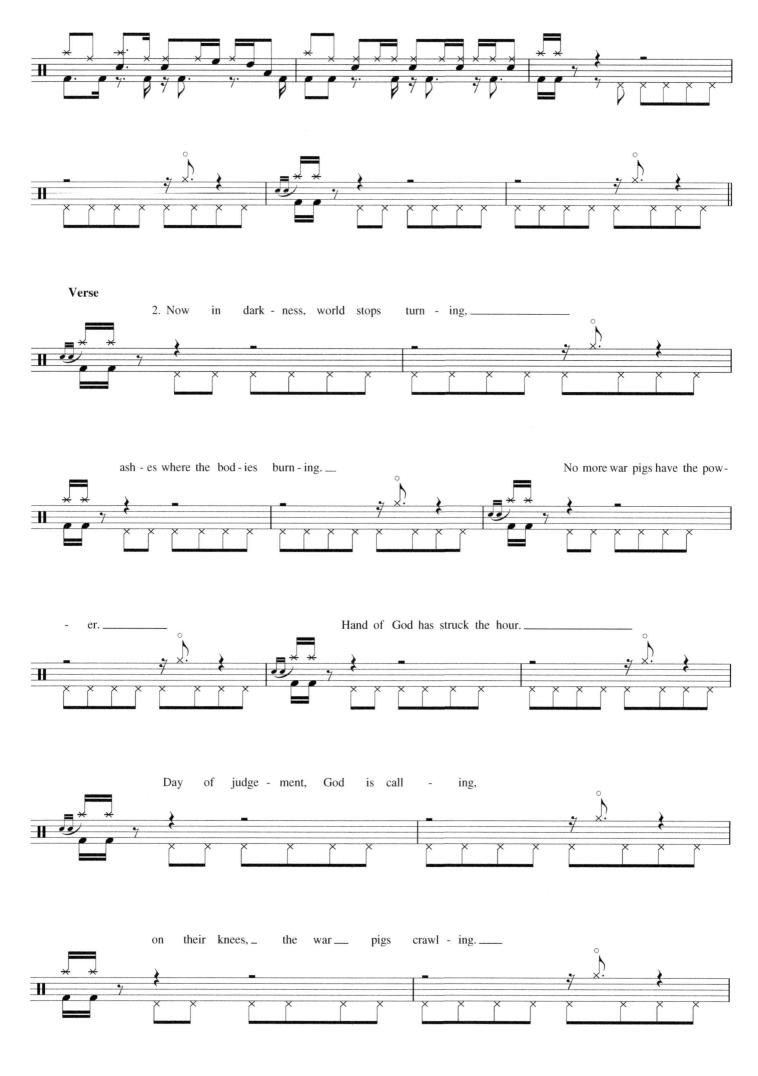

Verse

2. Now in dark - ness, world stops turn - ing, _____

ash - es where the bod - ies burn - ing. __ No more war pigs have the pow-

- er. _____ Hand of God has struck the hour. _____

Day of judge - ment, God is call - ing,

on their knees, __ the war __ pigs crawl - ing. __

Beg - ging mer - cies for their sins, _____

Sat - an laugh - ing, spreads his wings. _____ Oh, Lord, yeah.

Interlude

*accel.

*Tape speeds up.

DRUM PLAY-ALONG

AUDIO ACCESS INCLUDED

The Drum Play-Along™ Series will help you play your favorite songs quickly and easily! Just follow the drum notation, listen to the audio to hear how the drums should sound, and then play-along using the separate backing tracks. The lyrics are also included for reference. The audio files are enhanced so you can adjust the recording to any tempo without changing pitch!

HAL•LEONARD®

Visit Hal Leonard Online at
www.halleonard.com

Prices, contents and availability subject to change without notice and may vary outside the US.

DRUM TRANSCRIPTIONS
FROM HAL LEONARD

THE BEATLES DRUM COLLECTION
26 drum transcriptions of some of the Beatles' best, including: Back in the U.S.S.R. • Birthday • Can't Buy Me Love • Eight Days a Week • Help! • Helter Skelter • I Saw Her Standing There • Ob-La-Di, Ob-La-Da • Paperback Writer • Revolution • Sgt. Pepper's Lonely Hearts Club Band • Something • Twist and Shout • and more.
00690402 . . . . $19.99

BEST OF BLINK-182
Features Travis Barker's bashing beats from a baker's dozen of Blink's best. Songs: Adam's Song • Aliens Exist • All the Small Things • Anthem Part II • Dammit • Don't Leave Me • Dumpweed • First Date • Josie • Pathetic • The Rock Show • Stay Together for the Kids • What's My Age Again?
00690621 . . . . $22.99

DRUM CHART HITS
Authentic drum transcriptions of 30 pop and rock hits are including: Can't Stop the Feeling • Ex's & Oh's • Get Lucky • Moves like Jagger • Shake It Off • Thinking Out Loud • 24K Magic • Uptown Funk • and more.
00234062 . . . . $17.99

INCUBUS DRUM COLLECTION
Drum transcriptions for 13 of the biggest hits from this alt-metal band. Includes: Are You In? • Blood on the Ground • Circles • A Crow Left of the Murder • Drive • Megalomaniac • Nice to Know You • Pardon Me • Privilege • Stellar • Talk Shows on Mute • Wish You Were Here • Zee Deveel.
00690763 . . . . $17.95

BEST OF THE DAVE MATTHEWS BAND FOR DRUMS
Cherry Lane Music
Note-for-note transcriptions of Carter Beauford's great drum work: The Best of What's Around • Crash into Me • What Would You Say.
02500184 . . . . $19.95

DAVE MATTHEWS BAND – FAN FAVORITES FOR DRUMS
Cherry Lane Music
Exact drum transcriptions of every Carter Beauford beat from 10 of the most requested DMB hits: Crush • Dancing Nancies • Everyday • Grey Street • Jimi Thing • The Space Between • Tripping Billies • Two Step • Warehouse • Where Are You Going.
02500643 . . . . $19.95

METALLICA – ...AND JUSTICE FOR ALL
Cherry Lane Music
Drum transcriptions to every song from Metallica's blockbuster album, plus complete drum setup diagrams, and background notes on Lars Ulrich's drumming style.
02503504 . . . . $19.99

METALLICA – BLACK
Cherry Lane Music
Matching folio to their critically acclaimed self-titled album. Includes: Enter Sandman * Sad But True * The Unforgiven * Don't Tread On Me * Of Wolf And Man * The God That Failed * Nothing Else Matters * and 5 more metal crunchers.
02503509 . . . . $22.99

METALLICA – MASTER OF PUPPETS
Cherry Lane Music
Matching folio to the best-selling album. Includes: Master Of Puppets • Battery • Leper Messiah • plus photos.
02503502 . . . . $19.99

METALLICA – RIDE THE LIGHTNING
Cherry Lane Music
Matching folio to Metallica's second album, including: Creeping Death • Fade To Black • and more.
02503507 . . . . $19.99

NIRVANA DRUM COLLECTION
Features transcriptions of Dave Grohl's actual drum tracks on 17 hits culled from four albums: *Bleach, Nevermind, Incesticide* and *In Utero*. Includes the songs: About a Girl • All Apologies • Blew • Come as You Are • Dumb • Heart Shaped Box • In Bloom • Lithium • (New Wave) Polly • Smells like Teen Spirit • and more. Also includes a drum notation legend.
00690316 . . . . $22.99

BEST OF RED HOT CHILI PEPPERS FOR DRUMS
Note-for-note drum transcriptions for every funky beat blasted by Chad Smith on 20 hits from *Mother's Milk* through *By the Way*! Includes: Aeroplane • Breaking the Girl • By the Way • Californication • Give It Away • Higher Ground • Knock Me Down • Me and My Friends • My Friends • Right on Time • Scar Tissue • Throw Away Your Television • True Men Don't Kill Coyotes • Under the Bridge • and more.
00690587 . . . . $24.99

RED HOT CHILI PEPPERS – GREATEST HITS
Essential for Peppers fans! Features Chad Smith's thunderous drumming transcribed note-for-note from their *Greatest Hits* album. 15 songs: Breaking the Girl • By the Way • Californication • Give It Away • Higher Ground • My Friends • Scar Tissue • Suck My Kiss • Under the Bridge • and more.
00690681 . . . . $22.99

RED HOT CHILI PEPPERS – I'M WITH YOU
Note-for-note drum transcriptions from the group's tenth album: The Adventures of Rain Dance Maggie • Annie Wants a Baby • Brendan's Death Song • Dance, Dance, Dance • Did I Let You Know • Ethiopia • Even You Brutus? • Factory of Faith • Goodbye Hooray • Happiness Loves Company • Look Around • Meet Me at the Corner • Monarchy of Roses • Police Station.
00691168 . . . . $22.99

RUSH – THE SPIRIT OF RADIO: GREATEST HITS 1974-1987
17 exact drum transcriptions from Neil Peart! Includes: Closer to the Heart • Fly by Night • Freewill • Limelight • Red Barchetta • Spirit of Radio • Subdivisions • Time Stand Still • Tom Sawyer • The Trees • Working Man • 2112 (I Overture & II Temples of Syrinx).
00323857 . . . . $22.99

7777 W. BLUEMOUND RD. P.O. BOX 13819 MILWAUKEE, WI 53213
www.halleonard.com

0222
154

Prices, contents and availability subject to change without notice.